BOOK ONE
THE GOLDEN GAME

STEED AND MRS PEEL

BASED ON THE HIT TV SHOW 'THE AVENGERS'
WRITTEN BY
GRANT MORRISON
ILLUSTRATED BY
IAN GIBSON

ECLIPSE BOOKS·ACME PRESS

STEED AND MRS PEEL Book One

Published by
Eclipse Comics, P.O. Box 1099, Forestville, California 95436 USA
and
Acme Press, 391 Coldharbour Lane, London SW9 8LQ UK.

Writer:
Grant Morrison
Artist:
Ian Gibson
Letterer:
Ellie de Ville
Designer:
Rian Hughes
Editor:
Dick Hansom
Back Cover Photographer:
John R Ward
Consulting Editors:
Dave Rogers
Catherine Yronwode
Michael Bennent

Eclipse Comics:
Dean Mullaney, Publisher
Catherine Yronwode, Editor-In-Chief
Jan Mullaney, Chairman
Bruce Palley, Vice-President
Ted Adams, Circulation
Beau Smith, Sales Manager

Acme Press Editorial Board:
Richard Ashford
Katey Bird
Dick Hansom
Cefn Ridout

ISBN 1-870084-75-6

Printed in the USA.

part one

CROWN & ANCHOR

ЯОНЗИА & ИWORƆ

:ɘno ƚɿɒq

1

... STILL INVESTIGATING THE DEATH OF EVELYN GLASS, THE LONDON JEWELLER WHO WAS FOUND MURDERED AT HIS HOME TWO DAYS AGO ...

GLASS, WHO WAS STABBED SEVERAL TIMES WITH WHAT POLICE DESCRIBE AS A CHANDELIER CRYSTAL, WAS BEST KNOWN FOR HIS APPEARANCES ON TV'S 'ANTIQUES GANGSHOW' ...

TWO POUND THEN.

TWO POUND? YOU JUST COME BACK FROM THE POST OFFICE, YOU CAN DO BETTER THAN TWO POUND!

LAST OF THE BIG SPENDERS!

HAHAHA.

ALL RIGHT THEN ... A FIVER. A FIVER ON THE CROWN.

THAT'S MORE LIKE IT.

TWO POUND!

RIGHT! SHUT UP!

TWO POUND!

LOOK, I'M BANKER IN THIS GAME.

BANKER! NEARLY, MATE, NEARLY!

HAHAHA

WEYYYY!

THEM DICE IS RIGGED!

HAHAHAH

...WELL, A SMASHING DAY HERE IN LONDON BUT UN- FORTUNATELY IT'S NOT GOING TO LAST ONCE THAT TROUGH OF LOW PRESSURE COMES IN OVER THE CHANNEL...

MISS KING?

TARA KING?

SORRY I'M A LITTLE LATE; HAD A HARD TIME NAVIGATING THE WATERLOO BRIDGE. I'M FANSHAWE, BY THE WAY, ADMIRAL FANSHAWE.

'FOGGY' TO M'FRIENDS, 'FOGGY' TO MY ENEMIES. TAKE YOUR PICK.

OH, RIGHT... YES, YOU ARE A LITTLE LATE...

LATER THAN YOU THINK, MISS KING, BUT NOT SO LATE I CAN'T BE KNOCKED OFF MY SEA LEGS BY THE SIGHT OF A PRETTY YOUNG MISS LIKE YOUR- SELF.

SHALL WE?

IF YOU SAY SO...

...SO YOU'RE SAYING THAT SOMEONE'S BEEN LEAKING INFORMATION FROM MY DEPARTMENT?

ACCORDING TO OUR **SOURCES**, YES. IT SEEMS THAT YOUR **SECURITY** HASN'T BEEN QUITE AS EFFICIENT AS IT OUGHT TO BE.

THE WORD 'MOLE' HAS BEEN MENTIONED...

YOU MAY HAVE NOTICED THAT I'M A **NAUTICAL** MAN, MISS KING, AND WHERE I COME FROM 'LEAK' IS A NASTY WORD.

I RUN A TIGHT SHIP DOWN AT THE MINISTRY AND IF WE'RE SHIPPING WATER I WANT TO **KNOW** ABOUT IT.

WHAT I PLAN TO DO IS TAKE YOU DOWN TO THERE RIGHT NOW. WE'LL SOON HAVE THIS AFFAIR UNDER CONTROL.

'AND WE'LL ALL PULL TOGETHER...', WHAT? BLADE ON THE FEATHER AND ALL THAT.

WELL, I HOPE YOU'RE **RIGHT** BECAUSE OTHERWISE I CAN'T TELL **WHERE** ALL THIS MAY LEAD.

THIS **IS** RATHER **SERIOUS**, ADMIRAL FANSHAWE.

AH, DON'T YOU **WORRY**, MISS KING. I'VE SAILED STORMIER WATERS THAN THESE IN MY TIME.

AND AS FOR MOLES, I USUALLY **BRAIN** THE LITTLE DEVILS WITH MY SPADE.

'FOGGY'.

OH YES, IT'LL BE A LONG TIME BEFORE OLD 'FOGGY' FANSHAWE TAKES HIS PLACE AMONG THE DEAD IN DAVY JONES LOCKER.

A LONG TIME INDEED.

4

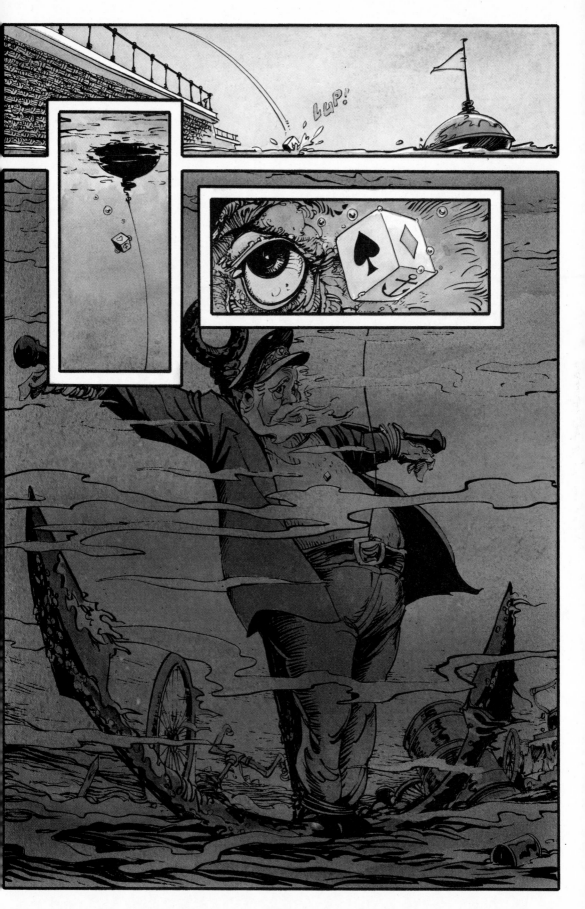

AFTERNOON.

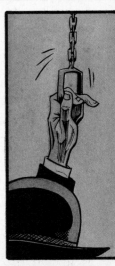

7

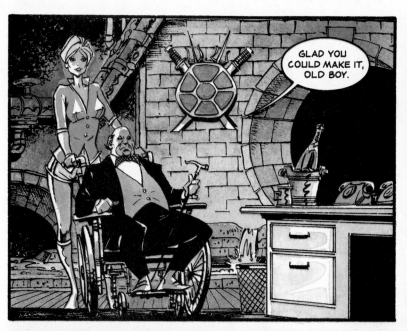

GLAD YOU COULD MAKE IT, OLD BOY.

AFTERNOON, MOTHER.

RATHER DAMP, DOWN HERE, DON'T YOU THINK?

DON'T BE SUCH A MILKSOP, STEED.

THE SITUATION, AS I'M SURE YOU'RE AWARE, IS CRITICAL. THE DEPARTMENT'S IN AN UPROAR AND WE HAVE A MOLE IN OUR MIDST. EVERYONE IS UNDER SUSPICION.

EVERYONE EXCEPT YOU, OLD CHAP. YOUR LOYALTY HAS NEVER BEEN IN DOUBT.

I AM, OF COURSE, DEEPLY CONCERNED ABOUT THE WELFARE OF MISS KING. SHE'S RASH AND IRRITATINGLY IMPETUOUS BUT I WOULDN'T WANT TO SEE HER COME TO ANY HARM. I SHOULDN'T HAVE ALLOWED HER TO MEET FANSHAWE ON HER OWN.

NO.

WHAT DO YOU WANT ME TO DO?

I WANT YOU TO LOOK INTO FANSHAWE'S DEATH! WHAT ELSE? THAT'S THE KEY TO ALL THIS UNPLEASANTNESS. BUT, REMEMBER, YOU'RE ALL ALONE IN THIS.

TRUST NO ONE, STEED.

YOU KNOW ME: I'M LIKE AN ABACUS, MOTHER.

GOOD SHOW, STEED! I KNEW I COULD COUNT ON YOU.

TAKE A LOOK AT THIS. THE DIVERS FOUND IT BESIDE FANSHAWE'S BODY.

IT'S PROBABLY NOTHING.

YES.

PROBABLY.

HA.

TRUST NO ONE, STEED.

TRUST NO ONE.

MRS PEEL?

WE'RE NEEDED.

THE GOLDEN GAME

...FOREVER AND EVER.

AMEN.

I REALLY WASN'T SURE IF YOU'D COME.

YOU MUST KNOW BY NOW THAT YOU'RE *IRRESISTIBLE*, STEED.

AND ANYWAY, I NEED THE EXCITEMENT AFTER SIX MONTHS AMONG THE LEOPARD PEOPLE OF THE AMAZON BASIN.

IT'S AN IMPRESSIVE TURNOUT I MUST SAY. I DIDN'T REALISE OLD 'FOGGY' HAD SO MANY FRIENDS.

HOW'S *MR PEEL*, BY THE WAY?

STILL IN THE AMAZON BASIN. HIS FRIENDS ASKED HIM TO STAY ON FOR SOME GRUESOME *CEREMONY* BUT HE'S PROMISED TO BE BACK FOR CHRISTMAS.

DO YOU STILL LIKE YOUR TEA STIRRED...?

OF COURSE.

YOU **DO** KNOW YOU'RE THE ONLY PERSON I CAN TRUST, MRS PEEL...

WHY, STEED, I'M DEEPLY TOUCHED.

WHATEVER HAPPENED TO THE NEW GIRL?

IT'S RATHER A LONG STORY. I'LL TELL YOU ON THE WAY.

SO WHAT'S THE GAMEPLAN?

WE PAY A VISIT CHEZ FANSHAWE, PICK UP THE CLUES, SOLVE THE MYSTERY...

AND BE BACK IN TIME FOR DINNER AT THE RITZ.

JUST LIKE OLD TIMES.

IT'S VERY... UNUSUAL...

WELL, APPARENTLY THE OLD BOY WAS RATHER ECCENTRIC BUT SOMETHING OF A WIZARD WHEN IT CAME TO DEVISING WARGAME STRATAGEMS.

IT'S THE ONLY REASON THEY KEPT HIM ON AFTER RETIREMENT AGE

YO HO HO.

AH... YOU MUSS BE THE... UMM...

YES, THAT'S US.

OH WELL... YOU'D BETTER COME IN THEN... RRUP...

'SCUSE ME.

HAVE YOU EVER THOUGHT ABOUT A CAREER IN MODELLING, MRS PEEL?

I DON'T THINK I HAVE THE TEMPERAMENT.

PITY. WE'RE ALWAYS ON THE LOOKOUT, YOU KNOW.

THAT'S NOT WHY I'M HERE, MS MANCHESTER. AS I SAID, I'D DESPERATELY LIKE TO HAVE A WORD WITH DORIS STORM.

I'M DEEPLY WORRIED ABOUT MY HUSBAND. AND...WELL, THERE'S ANOTHER MAN INVOLVED...

I SEE. WELL, SHE'S DOWN THERE, MRS PEEL. DORIS IS DOWN THERE.

WE'VE HAD THE BLOOD TRANSFUSION PEOPLE VISITING TODAY AND DORIS IS ALWAYS VERY KEEN TO DO HER BIT.

SHE'S DOWN THERE. THOUGH, FOR THE LIFE OF ME, I CAN'T IMAGINE *YOU* AS SOMEONE WHO COULD POSSIBLY HAVE ANY PROBLEMS.

WHAT?

SEE. YOU KNOW, YOU REALLY DO HAVE THE MOST WONDERFUL BONE STRUCTURE...

THAT'S THE TICKET. JUST LIE BACK AND MAKE YOURSELF COMFORTABLE.

HAVE YOU DONE THIS BEFORE?

OH, HUNDREDS OF TIMES.

I'VE BEEN GIVING BLOOD SINCE I WAS AT *COLLEGE*. I MUST HAVE DONATED A *LAKEFUL* IN MY TIME.

WELL, THAT'S THE SPIRIT. YOU WOULDN'T BELIEVE SOME OF THE MEN WE GET IN HERE. TALK ABOUT *SISSIES!*

WHICH REMINDS ME...

I HOPE YOU DON'T MIND, DORIS, BUT I'M A BIT WORRIED ABOUT MY BOYFRIEND...

THING IS, I FOUND THIS SUITCASE UNDER THE BED AND WHEN I OPENED IT, I FOUND THESE TRAVEL BROCHURES AND ITEMS OF HUNGARIAN NATIONAL DRESS. I JUST DON'T...

SHUUMNN
UH

WHAT
HAPPENED?

GIVE BLOOD, SAVE A LIFE!

SHE WAS SUPPOSED TO BE TAKING BLOOD BUT SHE INJECTED HER WITH SOMETHING.

HER PULSE IS SLOWING DOWN! WHAT AM I GOING TO DO? I'LL GET THE BLAME...

MISS STORM?

DORIS, CAN YOU HEAR ME?

...RUH-RUH-ROOKS...

...ROOKS AND... RAVENS...

ROOKS AND RAVENS?

part two:

HARE & HOUNDS

I WON'T REPEAT MYSELF AGAIN, SIR.

OUT!

BUT WAIT A MINUTE...

YOU HAVE NO RIGHT!

I'M ENTITLED TO JOIN THIS CLUB!

OUT.

I'VE SPENT YEARS! I'VE WASTED EIGHT YEARS OF MY LIFE ON THIS GAME!

YOU CAN'T JUST SHUT ME OUT WITHOUT A HEARING...

I'M SORRY. ENTRY IS RESTRICTED TO CLUB MEMBERS AND CLUB MEMBERSHIP IS RESTRICTED TO THE INVENTORS AND DESIGNERS OF GAMES.

EITHER YOU FIT INTO ONE OR BOTH OF THOSE CATEGORIES OR YOU TURN ROUND AND LEAVE, SIR.

BOARD GAMES, CARD GAMES, TEAM GAMES, ETCETERA, ETCETERA.

I SEE.

WELL, AS A MATTER OF FACT, I HAVE JUST INVENTED A NEW CARD GAME.

IT'S CALLED SUSPENSION BRIDGE. I'D LIKE TO...

THERE'S NO POINT TELLING ME WHAT IT'S CALLED, SIR.

YOU'LL HAVE TO BE NOMINATED BY AN EXISTING MEMBER.

THAT'S ALL RIGHT, BRADFORD.

I'M PROPOSING HIM FOR MEMBERSHIP.

OH... RIGHTO, MR BIRD.

WELL IN THAT CASE YOU'D BETTER COME IN, SIR.

I SUPPOSE I'D BETTER, HADN'T I?

YOU'LL HAVE TO EXCUSE ME WHILE I FETCH THE REQUIRED PAPER-WORK.

DIDN'T I SEE YOU AT 'FOGGY' FANSHAWE'S FUNERAL...?

SHH! KEEP YOUR VOICE DOWN.

I CAN'T TALK NOW...

MEET ME TOMORROW NIGHT, AFTER DORIS STORM'S FUNERAL, AT THE HARE AND HOUNDS PUB IN WHITE-CHAPEL...

AHUM.

YOUR APPLICATION FORM, SIR.

THAT'S IF YOU STILL WANT IT.

THE HARE AND HOUNDS PUB. TEN O' CLOCK.

OH, I WANT IT, ALL RIGHT.

I'M NOT JUST PLAYING GAMES, YOU KNOW.

DIGITALIS, PUMPED DIRECTLY INTO HER VEINS.

ACCORDING TO THE AUTOPSY THAT'S WHAT KILLED DORIS STORM.

IT STOPPED HER HEART IN MINUTES. THE NURSE WHO ADMINISTERED THE INJECTION IS IN A HOPELESSLY CONFUSED STATE AND SHE CAN'T REMEMBER WHY SHE DID IT.

DORIS STORM WAS ALSO THE INVENTOR OF THE 'LONELY HEARTS' BOARD GAME.

AND A CHARTER MEMBER OF THE PALAMEDES CLUB. FOR PEOPLE OBSESSED WITH GAMES OF CHANCE, THEY DO SEEM TO BE RATHER AN UNLUCKY BUNCH.

I WONDER WHAT SHE MEANT BY 'ROOKS AND RAVENS'.

IS IT A GAME, DO YOU THINK?

STEED?

HADN'T YOU BETTER ANSWER THE PHONE?

AH, MOTHER! ... YES, I DID HEAR THE TEST MATCH SCORES. A TRAGEDY... IT'S...

WHAT?

I SEE.

YES, SHE IS.

INVALUABLE, MOTHER ... YES. YES, I I UNDERSTAND...

BYE.

WELL?

THAT WAS MOTHER. IT TURNS OUT THAT FANSHAWE WAS WORKING ON SOMETHING CALLED 'HANGMAN' - A WARGAME PROGRAMME.

THE LEAKS HAVE BEEN TRACED DIRECTLY TO FANSHAWE'S OWN OFFICE.

AS PART OF HIS JOB, HE WAS ENTRUSTED WITH THE CODES WHICH ALLOW DIRECT, PRIVILEGED ACCESS INTO THE COMPUTERS THAT MONITOR AND CONTROL THE COUNTRY'S ARSENAL OF MISSILES.

NUCLEAR MISSILES, MRS PEEL.

31

...FORASMUCH AS IT HATH PLEASED ALMIGHTY GOD OF HIS GREAT MERCY TO TAKE UNTO HIMSELF THE SOUL OF OUR DEAR SISTER HERE DEPARTED, WE THEREFORE COMMIT HER BODY TO THE GROUND.

EARTH TO EARTH, ASHES TO ASHES, DUST TO DUST...

A HEART OF STONE FOR A HEART OF GOLD EVERYBODY'S FAVOURITE AUNTIE - DORIS STORM

'GONE TO SOLVE THE PROBLEMS OF THE ANGELS'

IN SURE AND CERTAIN HOPE OF THE RESURRECTION TO ETERNAL LIFE, THROUGH OUR LORD JESUS CHRIST.

WHO SHALL CHANGE OUR VILE BODY THAT IT MAY BE LIKE UNTO HIS GLORIOUS BODY, ACCORDING TO THE MIGHTY WORKING WHEREBY HE IS ABLE TO SUBDUE ALL THINGS TO HIMSELF.

I HEARD A VOICE FROM HEAVEN...

SIMON BIRD?

KNOWN TO MILLIONS AS THE 'CHAIRMAN OF THE BOARDGAME'. HE ALSO RUNS 'THE ROOKERY' NIGHTCLUB, HAUNT OF THE RICH AND FAMOUS.

AND, LIKE EVERYONE WE MEET THESE DAYS, HE'S...

A CHARTER MEMBER OF THE PALAMEDES CLUB.

OUR FATHER, WHICH ART IN HEAVEN, HALLOWED BE THY NAME. THY KINGDOM COME. THY WILL BE DONE, IN EARTH AS IT IS IN HEAVEN.

GIVE US THIS DAY OUR DAILY BREAD. AND FORGIVE US OUR TRESPASSES AS WE FORGIVE THEM THAT TRESPASS AGAINST US.

AND LEAD US NOT INTO TEMPTATION; BUT DELIVER US FROM EVIL.

AMEN.

33

'AND SOLLY-TEAR'S THE YONLY GAME IN TOWWWN... ANEVERRY ROAD IT TAKES IM TAKES IM DOWWWN...'

'AHDEEDEEE DEE DEEE DEEE DEE DE DAH...HE'S PLAYING SOLLY-TEAR...'

'AN SOLLY...'

...OH...

TWO OF CLUBS: YOU WILL MEET WITH OPPOSITION.

WHAT'S THAT? WHAT DID YOU...

AH

THREE OF CLUBS: A MEETING WITH A DEAR FRIEND THROUGH AN AUTOMOBILE RIDE.

FOUR OF CLUBS: DENOTES A CHANGE OF CONDITION OR POSITION.

HUKK!

FIVE OF CLUBS: NEWS FROM THE COUNTRY.

SIX OF CLUBS: YOU WILL RECEIVE GOOD ADVICE FROM A FRIEND.

SEVEN OF CLUBS: AN UN-LOOKED FOR CALLER.

BIRD?

BIRD!

BIRD, IT'S ME. IT'S STEED.

HOLD ON...

YOU! CALL AN AMBULANCE!

WHUT?

WHUT, ME? A WHUT?...

AN AMBLIANCE, IS THAT?

URM... HOW D'YOU SPELL IT?

37

'A flower blooms in every breast
That bears the gales of love
A flower stills the beating heart
In Reynard's velvet glove'

DORIS STORM.

THIS IS A REFERENCE TO DORIS STORM.

EXACTLY. AND DIGITALIS IS MORE COMMONLY KNOWN AS...

FOXGLOVE.

DO YOU BEGIN TO GET THE UNMISTAKABLE FEELING THAT EVERYTHING THAT'S HAPPENED HAS BEEN ORCHESTRATED?

HOW FAMILIAR ARE YOU WITH THE GAME OF CROWN AND ANCHOR, MRS PEEL?

IT'S A PUB GAME, PLAYED WITH DICE. INSTEAD OF NUMBERS, THE DICE ARE MARKED WITH SIX SYMBOLS — A CROWN, AN ANCHOR, A HEART, A CLUB, A SPADE AND A DIAMOND.

THIS WAS FOUND BESIDE 'FOGGY' FANSHAWE'S BODY. RING ANY BELLS?

THE ADMIRAL. ANCHOR. AND CROWN.

KING.

TARA KING.

HEART.

DORIS STORM.

CLUB.

SIMON BIRD.

AND DIAMOND.

40

EVELYN GLASS, THE **JEWELLER** WHO WAS FOUND DEAD TWO DAYS BEFORE **TARA** WENT MISSING.

YET ANOTHER CHARTER MEMBER OF THE PALAMEDES CLUB. I CHECKED.

WHICH LEAVES THE SPADE.

THE ACE OF SPADES?

DEATH?

THE GOLDEN GAME

Reynard's Riddles

I THINK WE'RE DEFINITELY ONTO SOME-THING, MRS PEEL.

BOTTOMS UP, MR STEED.

...THOU KNOWEST, LORD, THE SECRETS OF OUR HEARTS; SHUT NOT THY MERCIFUL EARS TO OUR PRAYER; BUT SPARE US, LORD MOST HOLY.

O GOD MOST MIGHTY, O HOLY AND MERCIFUL SAVIOUR, THOU MOST WORTHY JUDGE ETERNAL.

SUFFER US NOT, AT OUR LAST HOUR, FOR ANY PAINS OF DEATH, TO FALL FROM THEE.

TCHUKK!

SPADE.

TT!

GONE.

HE'S GONE.

BUT NOT FORGOTTEN.

LOOK.

WHAT IS IT? WHAT HAVE YOU FOUND, STEED?

A GAME.

ANOTHER GAME.

HANGMAN.

BOOM!

45

CONTINUED